You're On Your Own Little Girl

BY

Shelby Kane

Fiction Based On A True Story

This book is dedicated to those with no voice, and the children who once lived it

Forward

A raw and riveting account of childhood trauma, neglect, and adult betrayal.

Based during a time when childhood abuse went unnoticed. An era when children became adults at a young age to love, honor, serve, and protect their elders. This novella is fast paced, and will leave the reader in awe.

This story is told through the eyes and journal of the adult child who once lived it ~ Shelby Kane

Suggested Reading

F*Coping Start Healing and Beyond Anxiety

Dennis Simsek

It Didn't Start With You

Mar Wolynn

The Body Keeps The Score

Bessel Van Der Kolk

Freedom From Nervous Suffering

Claire Weekes

In The Beginning

Sometimes you have to tell your story, and especially when it hurts ~

I was an independent rebel with my back against the world. My way of showing people who I was, found me in a pair of worn out blue jeans, scuffed leather boots, and with my Daddy's guitar strapped over my shoulder. A slender young girl; my flowing brown hair loosely tucked behind my ears, and my deep brown eyes often hidden behind a pair of aviator glasses. I was a seventeen year old free spirit with so many dreams, but nowhere to go.

That's me, Shelby Kane, and this is the actual story of my life, my childhood trauma, and recovery.

My childhood had abruptly ended when I became an instant mother figure to my four young siblings;

That was when my parents divorced, and my Mother took flight with her newfound wings. By thirteen, my Mom finally decided to settle down again. Unfortunately, the only thing I ever got out of her new marriage was an A+ in abuse, with my new Stepfather, Johnny being the teacher.

It was early October, when Johnny and I had taken a ride through the cornfields of Ukron. We were on our way to pick up my baby sister Quinn. She had been visiting with her friend Sylvia. While bouncing around on the seat of the old pickup truck, I was keeping time to the song Afternoon Delight as it tried to play beneath the AM radio static. Gazing toward the half-plowed cornfield ahead, I noticed what I first thought was a scarecrow that had fallen from its mast, but in my split moment of question, Johnny had already slammed on the brakes. We both leapt out of the truck, and came upon him. It was Sylvia's father. His eyes were wide open, and he was staring straight up at me.

His heart decided that it had worked hard enough on that hot Indian Summer day.

His frozen facial expression, would forever be etched in my mind as he lay in state between the weathered rows of corn, and to this day, the smell of the diesel fuel from the tractor that he had been riding, still lingers in my senses. I will never listen to the song Afternoon Delight again.

My hands covered my ears, while I desperately tried to drown out the sorrowful moaning and screaming that echoed from the old farmhouse that day, as Johnny broke the news to the dead farmer's wife. I deeply felt her pain, as if it were my own.

I assumed my role and bravely pulled myself together to gather the children. I wasted no time, and swept them away to the old General Store for a popsicle, and by the time they were licking the sticky grape sugar off of their arms, the ambulance had already come and gone.

No child should witness tragedy, know abuse, or ever be put into any compromising adult situations. I had learned this lesson first hand, and now adding to my own personal list of childhood trauma, was death. However, something else I had seen that afternoon was much more disturbing to me. As Johnny leaned over the limp body of the dead farmer in the field, he carefully rolled him on his side, slipped his hand into the farmer's soiled back pocket, and removed his wallet. I tried to act as if I did not see him do it, but Johnny clearly saw me react. Yes, Johnny really did steal a dead man's wallet that day. I saw him do it!

That night at home was very quiet. Beneath the dim light of the parlor shone a veil of smoke, as my Mom, better known as Claire, sat in her black rocker chain smoking as she watched The Lawrence Welk Show with Johnny. My siblings were already in bed.

Not wanting to be heard, I silently took my boots off, and slipped down the basement stairs to my room.

Sleep didn't come too easy, as the vision of the dead farmer's face was still freshly planted in my mind.

Sometime thereafter, when I thought that the whole world was fast asleep, I was stunned and shaken as his cold hand snuck up on me, and abruptly ripped me out of bed by the roots of my hair. I did not hear him coming, and all I could see in the darkness were the whites of Johnny's eyes glaring deep into mine. I knew not to scream, and did not try to resist him. Johnny fiercely dragged me on my bare back across the concrete floor, and then dangled me by my neck. With a tight chokehold, he held me firmly against the drywall, and he was spitting venom in my face as he spoke "Girl, you ain't seen nothing"! With that said, he dropped my shaken body to the floor, and simply walked away.

I waited until I heard him reach the upstairs landing, and then slowly crawled my way back to bed. I cried hard that night, and as I picked the gravel out of my raw back, I wished for my real father to come home and rescue me.

My real Daddy was a very kind, gentle, and loving man. He was a Marine Corp. Veteran who had seen frontline combat in the Korean War. He married my mom when she was only sixteen, and he was ten years her senior. Mom on the other hand, although a beautiful woman, had dropped out of school in the 8th grade. She came from a troubled family in town that were labeled as "backward". Don't get me wrong…I loved my Mom, and I truly understood, and accepted her unknowing ignorance.

I often wondered why Daddy had abruptly vanished from our lives, but now I know that it wasn't his choice. It was Johnny who had kept him from us. Johnny was always ready to alert the Sheriff, who would then wait on the edge of town to pick Daddy up if he ever tried to breach the Ukron County limits. Johnny had the Sheriff convinced that Daddy was abusive. The truth was though…that Johnny was the abusive one. I had a regular diet of Johnny's fists, and his unkind verbal wisdom. He kept it well hidden, and if I were to tell anyone, they would have never believed me. Johnny had me portrayed as a troubled teen, and sowed his seeds about me to all of our relatives, neighbors, and friends.

An abused child feels like a burden…not only to themselves, but to their elders, and the people that surround them ~

Goodbye Mom

Finally! I became an honors graduate of the
Ukron County High School. I had always
planned on using my school diploma as my
ticket to freedom, and I desperately wanted to
attend college, but Johnny scolded me
whenever the subject would arise, and he
reminded me at least once a day that I was "Just
a jerk" who would amount to nothing. Besides, if
I did leave, who would protect my Brother, and
Sisters? Who would become Johnny's next
victim? Who would take care of Mom?

It was a very cool and cloudy afternoon. I
strolled into our dimly lit farmhouse with
confidence, as my Ukron High School diploma
confirmed my success. I was greeted by Johnny.
He had been waiting for me in the kitchen, and I
could tell by his tight lips, that he was agitated.
"Oh…dear God, please don't let him ruin this
perfect day"!

I stood before him, smiled, and nervously asked him if I could make him a cup of coffee, or help start dinner for the little ones. Instead of answering, he gave my Mom a holler, and told her that he and I were going on an errand together, and then he quickly ushered me away. Here I was again…back in Johnny's truck. He told me that we were going for a run to the town dump, but I noticed that there was no rubbish in the truck's bed. This caused a silent panic to settle in as we proceeded down the dusty old road ahead. Johnny didn't speak to me, nor did I speak to him. I could see that he was seething inside. I felt my heart pounding through my chest, and started to sweat. What did I do this time? I thought, as I tried to control my anxious panic.

Johnny skillfully backed his truck into the landfill, and then screamed at me to get out. I was so frightened that I nervously obliged, while realizing that I was his trash. With all of his force, and without time for me to react…he lunged at me, and kicked me hard in the stomach. I was sent swiftly rolling down the dark gulley below, and into the large heap of community garbage. The wind was knocked out of me, and I felt crushed by the shards of broken glass as they sharply pierced my body on my way to the bottom of hell.

I heard Johnny's truck peeling off in the distance, and as I layed among the caustic pile of debris, I asked myself…"What did I do to deserve this"? Using my backside and elbows, I struggled to make my way back up to the top of the dump landing. I was trying to be brave, as I thought that this might have been as painful as my Daddy's Marine days in the Korean War.

The sky was now completely black, and I knew it was a long way back to the main road, but I saw one light glowing in the distance, and decided to follow it. I knew it would lead me to the intersection. With a lot of determination, I dragged myself to the side of the dirt roadway, and proceeded cautiously.

I can't say that it took me all night, but it was in the wee hours of the morning when I finally arrived at the four corners.

My body slumped to the ground at the old railroad crossing, and to this very day, I don't remember how help came, only that it was the next afternoon when I awoke at Ukron General Hospital. I was surrounded by the Doctor, the Sheriff, my Mom, and Johnny.

My brain was in such a spacey fog due to the trauma, and the pain medication that I was given, but somehow I had to rally. I had to think fast. I had to concoct a believable story of how this could have happened to me without revealing my abuser.

I knew at that very moment that I was not protecting Johnny, but I was protecting my Mom, the one who never protected me. The one who was supposed to love me unconditionally, and yes…the same person, who sat in that black chair every day chain smoking cigarettes, and doing nothing except worrying about Johnny.

I told the authorities that I had gone out walking that day, and ended up at the town dump. I accidentally slipped over the edge of the landing. I knew I shouldn't have been there, and I was very sorry to have worried everyone.

I don't know why they all believed me, but they did. I looked deep into Johnny's eyes as I spun my sad tale, and I felt that if Johnny and I were alone, he probably would have killed me…literally.

To this very day, I still don't understand what I ever did to provoke Johnny's violent tirades.

I asked the Sheriff if I could have a moment alone to talk to my Mom. I laid in the hospital bed with three broken ribs, abrasions, and stitches throughout my body. I watched as the IV bag dripped ever so slowly into my arm, while getting the courage up to speak to her. My Mom sat in the chair next to me.

I asked her why she had allowed her husband to physically abuse me all these years. She showed no emotion, and as if she were numb to it all, she replied, "Because you are my daughter, and you will always love me…Johnny is my second husband, and I can't afford to lose another one". At least my Mom was being honest with her feelings that day. I wished instead that she had said I'm sorry Shelby, and I love you.

This was as deep as my Mom could get. She was completely hollow. I announced to her that I was leaving home. I told her how much I loved her, and that I always would. I left the Ukron Hospital one week later. I went home just long enough to gather my belongings, and as I walked out the door, I swore to myself that I would never spend another night in that farmhouse again!

Uncle Daniel

The only phone number and address I carried
with me when I left home that day belonged to
my Uncle Daniel, he was my Daddy's brother.
He lived in Maine, so I set my sights on heading
to the East Coast, and started walking. One day
at a time was my new motto, and my goal for the
first day was to get out of Ukron, and call my
Uncle from the next town. I had not spoken to,
nor seen Uncle Daniel in years. I remembered
him as a very stern man. I recall his long lean
stature, and how he would intimidate me. He
would always bend over to pat my head in the
same authoritative way the Priest used to pat my
head at Sunday Church service when I was just
a little girl.

The smell of stale coffee lured me into the
remote diner. I was so exhausted, and needed
to take my pain medication.

I had packed several sandwiches for my journey, and I had to make what little bit of money I had stolen from Johnny's wallet last. As I handed the waitress a dollar bill to pay for my coffee that day, I prayed that it had not been a dollar bill that Johnny had taken from the dead farmer's wallet.

With my coffee in hand, I clumsily grabbed hold of the soiled black phone handle, and nervously dialed his number. "Uncle…Please answer"! "This is Daniel" he responded. "Hello, Uncle Daniel, This is Shelby, I don't know where my Daddy is, but I had your phone number…Uncle…please, I need your help"! Without hesitation, he asked me where I was, and told me to stay right there. He sent a cab for me, and it picked me up outside the old diner later that night. It seemed like such a long ride, and I dozed off a time or two. I awoke to the commotion of the city. The cab driver pulled into the hotel's valet area, and helped me with my guitar, and bag.

He said that my Uncle Daniel had already paid the cab fare, as he yelled good luck, and sent me on my way.

When I entered the fine hotel, I thought that I must be dreaming. Everything around me sparkled, and was polished just so. My nose followed the scent of fine men's cologne all the way to the front desk, and I gave the young gentleman standing there my name. I let him know that my Uncle Daniel had sent me, and without another word, I was escorted upstairs to a luxury suite. This hotel was something that I had only seen while watching TV through my mom's veil of cigarette smoke. There was a typed note from Uncle Daniel on the dresser, and the concierge told me that I could order anything I wanted to eat. A menu was strategically seated beside a box of fancy chocolates, and atop of the plush king sized bed.

The note from Uncle stated that he was going to pick me up the next morning with his own private plane, and fly me back to his home on the East Coast. I layed in bed, and cried. I thought that perhaps I should have made this call a long time ago, but I was also crying for my losses…all of my siblings were back in Ukron. I vowed at that moment, no matter what happened in my future, that I was going to rescue them, the same way that Uncle had just rescued me. Quinn, Sarah, Flossie, and Brad. I could not bear the thought of any one of them suffering at Johnny's hand.

I awoke early the next morning to a hard knock on the hotel suite door. I squinted my eye and looked through the tiny glass peephole while swallowing hard. It was Uncle Daniel. He still had that stern face, just as I remembered, and every childhood memory of him instantly came flooding back to me.

I slowly opened the door, and looked up at him with a timid smile. He simply patted me on the head, and asked me if I were okay.

There was no way to hide the residual bruises and cuts that remained on my body, and face since my recent run-in with Johnny, and my broken ribs were still painfully wrapped. As Uncle Daniel entered the suite, I broke down, and while trying to hide my tears I asked him "Where is my Daddy "? Uncle said that there would be plenty of time for talking, as he caringly wrapped his arm around me, and led me out of the room. There were hardly any words spoken between us, but I had my Uncle Daniel sized up perfectly.

We boarded his private plane, and we were East Coast bound in no time at all. I was met by my new Aunt Samantha, and my two little twin Nephews, Anton, and Alton. Aunt Sam was wearing a long fur coat, and was dripping in gold jewelry. She seemed very sweet, and she welcomed me with a tight hug. She smiled, and told me it was going to be nice to have another woman in the house. As we walked from the plane together, I thought that I really liked Aunt Sam.

We would probably bond, and become good friends. I wondered though, what had become of my Aunt Kay, and her 6 children?

Changes

What I thought was the road leading to their house, was actually their long graceful driveway. When we turned the corner and approached, I was awestruck. I'd never seen a house as big as Uncle Daniel & Aunt Sam's. It was even larger than the Ukron Church.

Upon arrival, I was led upstairs into what would be my very own bedroom. Aunt Sam brought me some fresh clothing, and told me that she and Uncle would take me shopping the next day.

I unzipped my travel bag, and removed my favorite worn jeans, and my old leather boots, and tucked them away. It was as if I was saying goodbye to my old friends. I sensed my life was about to change for good.

The next morning I awoke to the aroma of pancakes, eggs, and bacon. I followed my nose to the bottom of the stairs to find the family already eating. I smiled, and instantly felt as if I had always belonged, as I dug into my plate of home cooked morning splendor.

I watched my Uncle as he relaxed on the couch after breakfast, and nervously tried to read his mood over the edge of his morning newspaper. He must have felt my urgency for our much needed conversation that morning, because he soon lowered his paper, cleared his throat, and started to speak.

He said, "Shelby, your Dad is out of the country on Real Estate business, and I'm unable to contact him". "He's expected to be away for the rest of the year". I needed my Daddy very much, but I sadly accepted this. I was drawn in by my

Uncle's likeness of Daddy, and hung on to him like a crutch, as he proceeded to speak.

Uncle Daniel really did open up to me that day.

He told me about his divorce from Aunt Kay, and how he had lost touch with his children because they did not approve of his second marriage, but now it was my turn to talk. I spilled the truth about Johnny to him, as he listened intently.

I told him I was very frightened for my Brother and Sisters back home, and also how I was even more frightened that Johnny might come looking for me. He would drag me out of my new found solace, and make me pay for my happiness. Uncle assured me that it was over. I would never suffer at Johnny's hand again, and that he would see to it that my siblings wouldn't either. He promised, and then reached over, and hugged me tight. Uncle Daniel and I have bonded.

My 18th Birthday arrived, and I thought it best not to mention it. I felt it would go better unnoticed, but after an early dinner, Uncle Daniel & Aunt Sam called me outside. Sitting on the edge of their manicured lawn sat my very first car. "Surprise"! They both wished me a Happy Birthday, and I kissed them both on their cheeks, and thanked them. I was in awe, and honestly, I loved all the attention I was getting, and the car was quite a bonus.

Needless to say, I was anxious to go for my first spin, as I eagerly slid behind the wheel. I drove along the coast until sunset that day, while taking in the beauty of my surroundings and enjoying my freedom.

As I drove, my thoughts became consumed with my family back in Ukron. I missed them dearly, and could not get them out of my head.

I used to shed my emotions alone in my bedroom, but today I have found a new place for my tears…in my little black sports car.

Rose

Several weeks later, and after a lot of contemplating, I hesitantly picked up the telephone and dialed the Ukron exchange. I wanted to let Mom know that I was okay, but at the same time, did not want Johnny to know that I called. On the fourth ring, she picked up. "Hello Mom, it's me Shelby". I let her know that I was safe, and told her how much I loved her.

Not once did I let on to her where I was living. I asked her about the children, and she said they were all doing fine, but I could tell by the broken tone in her voice that something was seriously wrong.

Mom talked more to me in that 3-minute call than she had ever spoken to me before. "It's Johnny," she said. "Brad found him out in the field, and he was badly beaten". "His neck is nearly broken, and his leg's mangled so severely that he will probably never be able to walk again". I told Mom that I was so very sorry, even though I felt no emotion for him at all.

Johnny was no longer a threat to me or my siblings. Was it God's wrath, or answered prayers?

After I hung up the phone, I ran straight to Uncle Daniel to let him know about Johnny. He sat at his desk, and barely lifted his head from his business upon hearing the news. I walked away from him thinking of how he had told me that Johnny would never hurt me ever again. I pondered…just how powerful was Uncle Daniel? Some things are better left unsaid.

I was intending on putting the money that I had taken from Johnny's wallet into the collection basket at Church on Sunday, but now I decided to send it to Mom instead. Perhaps this was how I could repent for my vengeful thoughts, and unkind prayers.

Most mornings, I would join Uncle Daniel and Aunt Sam on their daily business ventures. Uncle owned the Little Harbor Professional Building, along with several other buildings in the area. The Little Harbor Professional Building housed the Doctor, Dentist, and other small town businesses.

One morning after my Uncle Daniel had collected his monthly rent checks; we proceeded to our next stop, and soon approached the grand old resort house on the cliffs. It looked as if it had once been a landmark resort, and stood alone like a historic monument, facing the Atlantic Ocean.

We entered the old lobby, and all that remained were a few sparse antique furnishings, and the brass room keys that were hanging on the wall behind an oak desk. I noticed a dim light down a distant hall, as I started to hear the sound of a yapping dog, and from the shadows she slowly appeared with her regal little mate in tow.

Her name was Rose, and after she said hello to me, she said "Say hello to Shelby, Skipper". The little dog's tail started to wag. I was only slightly annoyed by Skipper's continual yapping, but my Uncle Daniel felt interrupted, and plainly showed his frustration with Rose's mate Skipper.

Rose on the other hand was the most beautifully kept older woman I had ever seen. A woman like her should be smiling, but I clearly sensed her loneliness.

Rose had known my Uncle Daniel for many years, and trusted him. He had his sights set on buying that old Resort House of hers one day, and would check in with her from time to time hoping for the day that she would sell. At least that is what Aunt Sam told me.

Today…Rose told Uncle Daniel that indeed, it was time for her to sell her diamond by the sea, and that she wanted to relocate to Florida.

Rose then handed Uncle a handful of colorful pamphlets that she had collected of the many beautiful ocean front condominiums that she liked on the Southeast coast of Florida. Uncle took Rose's hands in his, and assured her that he would personally oversee her resort house restoration, and then purchase the grand property from her, so she could buy the home of her dreams.

Soon after, Rose and her dog Skipper became frequent company, and regular dinner guests at our home. Aunt Sam found the sweet spot in Rose's heart, as she would accompany Rose on the piano, while she crooned old show tunes. Uncle would always put a dish of fresh ground sirloin out for Skipper when they arrived…not only to curb his regal appetite, but mostly to curb his incessant yapping.

With every one of Rose's visits, she grew on me more and more. I eventually began to love her, and treat her as if she were the Grandmother figure that I never had. She was filling a void in my heart without even knowing it. It was very sad to find out that Rose was a lonely spinster.

The Resort House

One morning while we were out on our daily rounds, my Aunt Sam and Uncle Daniel insisted that I see the local Doctor for a physical exam. It had been several months since I had left Ukron, and I never did have my ribs checked again. Besides that, I seemed to be living on nerves, and crying a lot without my Brother, and Sisters.

It was early one morning when we arrived at the professional building. I did not have a scheduled appointment as I walked to the door marked Internal Medicine, but seeing my Uncle owned the building, he said that the Doctor would surely see me.

Although the Doctor did give me a clean bill of health, he also gave me a prescription for a medicine he said would help calm my nerves. The medicine was a barbiturate called Librium.

We filled my prescription, and I washed a pill down with my last sip of coffee.

After a short while, I began to feel strange inside. Similar to the way I felt taking the pain medication that I was given while at the Ukron Hospital. I decided not to say anything, but never took the pills again, and I tossed the bottle into the bottom of my purse.

The sale of Rose's resort house was coming closer to reality. Uncle flew Rose down to the Florida Coast on his private plane, and she selected a beautiful ocean front condominium. Uncle Daniel assured her that he would handle the monetary details for her. He also said that he would personally move her, Skipper, and all of their belongings into their new home when the time came.

We spent nearly every day checking in on the progress of the old resort house as it was being restored to its old glory, and it was surely regaining its original charm.

Even the carriage house was making a grand comeback. That was where Rose kept her car, and after some snooping, I found that the rafters held many boxes of her personal childhood treasures.

I climbed the shaky old ladder to the eaves one day, and rummaged through many old trunks filled with antique ephemera. I also discovered Rose's colorful past through her childhood photographs. I enjoyed holding her porcelain dolls as I pictured her running through the lobby of the resort as a small child, with the dolls in tow.

Two weeks later, we went to pick up Rose again, and take her to lunch. My Uncle discussed the progress of the resort house restoration, and he assured Rose that he just secured the oceanfront condominium of her dreams, and that it was ready and waiting for her arrival south. He said that he thought in two months time, that she and little Skipper would be permanent residents of the sunshine state.

Rose was so excited, and I was very happy for her. Uncle held her hand, and with his trusting smile, she believed him.

We drove Rose home that day, and while saying our goodbyes, I offered to come see her the next day to help finish packing. She kissed me on the cheek, and thanked me for my kindness.

Our daily routine had become very intense now. My Uncle would barely let Rose out of his sight, and quickly closing the deal on the resort house was the only thing on his mind. He wanted those papers signed!

Uncle even insisted on buying Rose a new dress. He said that we would be taking her out for a celebration dinner fit for a queen when it was time for her to go.

One evening, soon after Rose and Skipper arrived for dinner, Uncle Daniel pulled me aside. He asked me if he could have some of the pills that the Doctor had given me for my anxiety and nerves.

He said that although he loved Rose, he just couldn't take Skipper's incessant yapping anymore, and that he just wanted to calm the little dog down a bit.

I was shocked, and I sternly yelled "No"! I knew giving him the pills was wrong, and I boldly told him so, but at the same time, my Uncle Daniel intimidated me with his authoritative ways, and he knew exactly what buttons to push with me. I became so afraid that if I didn't comply with him, I just might find myself out on the street again, and this time…without a number or person to call for help. I was shaking inside, and starting to have flashbacks of Johnny and his violent cruelty. Uncle assured me that the pills would not hurt the little dog in any way.

I hesitantly reached deep into my purse, and threw the unused bottle of pills directly at him as I walked away. I watched him later from the kitchen doorway, as he sprinkled the contents of a capsule on the little dog's fresh ground sirloin.

Covert manipulation is quite frightening, and the abusers tactics are scary enough to silently entice the victim to do whatever the manipulator wants, while taking advantage of their fragile emotional state, and vulnerability ~

I had never heard Aunt Sam, and Uncle Daniel argue before, but I overheard them in their bedroom late that night. Aunt Sam was firmly asking Uncle what he was going to do. She told him that he was supposed to be leaving with Rose for Florida soon, and said that she had no idea how he was going to pull it all off. She said she would be staying home with the twins, and wanted nothing to do with any of it.

Uncle was clearly irritated, and told her that it would all work out. "Don't worry about it"! he assured her.

I had most of Rose's belongings carefully packed into the carriage house, and ready for the big trip. While I was sitting up in the loft one day, I asked Rose about the old trunk, and her antique dolls. She watched as I carefully dragged the old leather trunk to the edge of the loft, and slowly lowered it down. She took the dolls out, and studied each one. She looked at them as if they were long lost friends, and then handed them to me. She gave me a hug, and told me that I had become very dear to her. She said she would be so happy if I would accept them as a special gift between her and I. We both had tears in our eyes, as I assured her that they would be treasured forever.
I set the dolls down ever so carefully in the back of my little black sports car, and strapped their little porcelain bodies into the seatbelts as if they were precious little babies.

Skipper

One more week until Rose's big move. There were papers to sign, a trailer to load and then…there was poor little Skipper. He had become ill this past week. Rose took him to the local Veterinarian, who decided that it would be best to admit Skipper to the Animal Hospital for testing.

Nobody seemed to be able to help the listless little dog, or know exactly what was wrong with him. Only my Uncle and I knew the truth of what ailed Skipper. I would never forgive myself if anything happened to dear Rose's little furry companion, and I especially wouldn't forgive my Uncle Daniel. Rose continued to be optimistic. She prayed that Skipper would be well enough for the trip south. I was thankful that this busy week would help keep her mind off her ailing best friend.

The day was finally here. Uncle Daniel sat behind his desk, as Rose sat across from him. I watched their business from afar as she finally signed the newly renovated resort house over to him. They must have signed a hundred papers that day. No money had changed hands yet, due to the fact that Uncle had just purchased a new oceanfront condo for Rose in Florida. He told Rose that once they were in Florida, that he would then sign the new condominium over to her, and present her with a bank check for the monetary discrepancy, minus the moving expenses. He assured her that she and Skipper would be set for life, and she trusted him.

Rose sat before him smiling. The papers were now signed, and the deal was done.

Rose told me again later on that day, how she had always wanted to see the old resort in its full glory, and now it looked as majestic as it once stood, and as it was originally depicted in the fine oil painting that hung over the mantle in her formal parlor. Now it was all that, and she did.

I took the fine painting off of the wall, and carefully packaged it up for her trip south. It was the very last thing I did for her.

The next day was busy. I had to watch the twins for Aunt Sam. She was out running errands for my Uncle Daniel. What I really wanted was to be visiting with Rose. I wanted to spend every moment I could with her before her move.

I was trying to prepare dinner for the boys, while dodging their little toy cars that they rolled recklessly across the kitchen floor. Eventually, Uncle Daniel walked into the house.

He had been gone most of the day. He approached me, and with a very concerned tone in his voice, he asked me if I had seen Rose.

I told him that I hadn't seen her all day, which led him to ask if I would go check on her after I fed the twins, because he had already been to the resort house three times that day, and she hadn't answered the door. I was starting to get frightened.

Uncle told me that Rose was probably at the Animal Hospital with Skipper, but asked me again if I would please check in on her. He mentioned that he had an important meeting at the Professional Building, and that he would meet me at the resort house after he was through.

Dinner was served, and I was very anxious to get to Rose.

Aunt Sam finally came through the door, and with a quick hello, and good-bye, I hopped into my car, and was on my way.

The Carriage House

I arrived at the resort house, and approached the door. The first thing I noticed was that three of Uncle Daniel's business cards were wedged behind the large brass knocker. He had said that he had been there three times that day. I turned the door handle, but it was locked. I started to panic, because Rose had never locked the door before, and we were always free to come and go as we pleased. Skipper would yap, and I would always see the dim light down the dark hall. Now it was quiet, the door locked, and not a flicker of light anywhere.

The carriage house was my first thought, and I hurriedly made my way back to my car to grab my flashlight. I then jogged back down the hill. I tugged hard to lift the heavy wooden carriage house door, but at first it would not budge.

With my flashlight in hand I shined it through the carriage house window, and there sat Rose's car, and the driver's door was open.

As I lowered the flashlight down towards the ground, there she lay...my dear Rose.

Her face was frozen, her eyes were wide open, and she was staring straight up at me.

"Dear God, this could not be happening"! I tripped over myself while running back to the car and by the time I made it to the Police Station; I was completely hysterical.

I was briefly questioned while being escorted back to the resort house in a police cruiser. Several other red and blue flashing lights passed us along the way.

I did not want to see Rose like that again, and I was purely in a state of shock. I so wanted to remember her new found joy, and her final weeks in the resort house.

I wrapped myself in a blanket, and perched myself on the cliffs as I cried. The vision of Rose would forever haunt me now, just like the dead farmer in the field.

I was eventually approached by a policeman, who was casing the property, and he asked me if I were Rose's next of kin, and I proudly replied…"Yes sir, I am". Nobody should die alone. Nobody.

What seemed like a long time was actually only minutes. I noticed Uncle Daniel's car coming up the gravel driveway. I watched him as he ran to the commotion of the carriage house, and I swiftly went after him. "Uncle Daniel, Rose is gone"! I yelled. He barely lifted his head from his chest, and did not say a word. The last time I had seen this reaction from Uncle, was when I had told him that Johnny had been beaten.

I listened as my Uncle Daniel was interrogated by the authorities. He told the Detectives that he had been at the house three times that day, and Rose hadn't answered the door. He also spoke as if she were very frail. He spoke of how he had just purchased the resort house from her, and that he was letting her stay on "his" property until she had found a new place to relocate to.

That very sad day I heard the truth. My Uncle Daniel made no mention whatsoever of Rose's little yapping dog Skipper (who was sick, and conveniently not on the premises that day), or of the new Florida oceanfront condo that he had promised he had bought her.

We held a formal wake, and funeral for Rose, and the dress that Uncle had bought Rose for our celebration dinner, was now on her lifeless body as she lay in her final state. Only a sparse number of people came to pay their respects, and bid Rose farewell that day.

Uncle Daniel, Aunt Sam, and I sat solemnly beside Rose's coffin to mourn. I happened to glance up as two stoic men walked in, both dressed in steel gray suits.

I was trying to size them up, while wondering how they knew Rose, when they suddenly approached me, and flashed their brass badges. I was asked to follow them upstairs. They were FBI agents.

I made eye contact with Uncle Daniel, as I walked up the stairs, and watched as his face turned from gray to white. The same way that Johnny's once did.

The two agents asked me many questions regarding their investigation into Rose's death. I told them in careful detail how I had found Rose laid out on the carriage house floor. I confirmed to them that Uncle Daniel had purchased the resort house from her days earlier. I stuck to the facts, and offered them nothing more.

There was never any accountability with Uncle Daniel and all of his callus, deceitful, and calculated acts made me think that he had no conscience at all…or was I just imagining what was right before me.

The Aftermath

I wore my white gauze dress with the pink ribbon sash to Church that Sunday. I was having suspicious thoughts about Uncle Daniel, and wanted to repent for using that convenient "Unknowing Ignorance" excuse again.

I found myself looking at Uncle in a completely new light now, and I was frightened that he would notice how I could see right through him.

According to the autopsy report, it was determined by the LH County Coroner that there were several factors that contributed to Rose's death. She had a contusion to her head, had suffered cardiac arrest, and also had a toxic level of carbon monoxide in her blood. It was concluded by the investigators involved that Rose had probably started her car, and then gotten out (leaving the car door open) to walk around to the back of the vehicle, and open the carriage house door.

The detectives deduced that she most likely had her heart attack at the rear of the vehicle, during her effort to lift the heavy overhead door and fell; therefore hitting her head on the floor. She was left lying unconscious by the tail pipe, and asphyxiated herself breathing in the monoxide from her running car. Case closed.

I took a stand, and went straight to the Animal Hospital first thing Monday morning, and without asking my Uncle…I paid for Skipper's hospital stay. I proudly discharged the little yapping dog. Rose would have been happy to know that Skipper was well again. He was mine now, and I would love him, and take care of him, in the same way that she had. Uncle Daniel was not thrilled when I came home with the little dog, but never said a word. Our eyes locked in the entryway, and I got his silent approval. I then asked if I could go to the resort house to gather some of Rose's personal items, and he agreed. He knew I loved her so.

I reached the front door of the resort house, and turned the handle. It was open this time, as it always had been in the past.

Little Skipper lept from under my arm, and bee lined down the long dark hallway. He was looking for Rose.

I took one last look around the place, and wiped my tears when I left. I had only taken one item from the main house that day. It was the fine mantle painting of the resort house in its original glory, the one I had just carefully wrapped and packed days earlier.

I then made my way down the hill to the carriage house. I was apprehensive, and afraid that the image of Rose's frozen face would come back to haunt me, but I swallowed hard, and mustered up enough courage to lift open the door. I climbed the old ladder to take one last look in the eaves, and slid the last old leather trunk that had been hiding in a corner, and lowered it down. It was when I dragged the old trunk towards the carriage house door that I noticed the wooden antique croquet set. All of the colored croquet mallets were still carefully preserved in their original holder except for one. It must have been 50 years since it had been played with…or was it?

My hair was standing on the back of my neck, as I hurriedly dragged the old trunk outside, and shut the door forever.

I would never go into the old carriage house again.

I opened the vintage trunk in the daylight, and sat on the cliffs savoring through the many old photographs of Rose's past.

Skipper, unknowingly was enjoying one of his last romp through the yard. I said my goodbyes to Rose in this way, and on my own terms…even though my thoughts of Rose would remain within me forever.

The Invasion

I had trouble adjusting to life with Uncle Daniel, and Aunt Sam after Rose's death. I no longer wanted to spend time with them on their morning business rounds, and I took dinner to my room most every evening. There were no more nights of singing at the piano, and the only happiness in the house came from Skipper, and the twins.

That Sunday at Church, I watched Uncle Daniel as he walked to his usual pew in the front row. I sat next to him, and wondered if he was praying or repenting.

I started thinking about my Mom, and how she lived silently in her black chair for so many years. Perhaps she harbored too many secrets, and like myself now, she was just a silent victim. Perhaps she was actually smarter than anyone I had ever known.

Don't play victim to circumstances created by others. It will set a precedent for how you label yourself today...victim mentality ~

I was done living a life of abuse, and deceit. The only normalcy I ever had was when my Daddy was a part of it. I needed him desperately, and finally decided to find out exactly where he was, and contact him on my own. I had to find a way. I needed so badly to cry on his shoulder, tell him about Johnny, Mom, the kids, the farmer in the field, Uncle Daniel, and Rose.

Aunt Sam and Uncle Daniel packed up for a day trip with the twins. I told them that I didn't feel well, and was going to stay at home. I watched their car as it slowly rolled out of the driveway, and did not lose a moment.

I easily unlocked Uncle Daniels office door with the edge of my license, and peeked my way in.

I went straight to it, and carefully read through every letter, and document. I found no information on Daddy, and nothing about the supposed overseas business trip that had been keeping him from me. Oh...and the southern oceanfront condominium that Uncle had told Rose that he had purchased for her…never was! It was nothing more than the pamphlet that she once proudly clutched in her hands.

I found one other document that piqued my curiosity that day; it was an agreement for Uncle Daniel's pending sale of the resort house.

According to the papers, my Uncle would be selling the resort house within the next 30 days. I thought about how he never did pay Rose for her house, and about his shallow ruthlessness. Uncle Daniel was no better than Johnny.

Every thought I was having about Uncle must be true! I left every paper exactly as I found it, and left no evidence of my office invasion.

I crept to the master suite to search through Uncle's armoire where he kept all of his personal belongings. I opened up his jewelry box, and saw several sets of business keys, and a few old pictures of his children from his past marriage to Aunt Kay. Just when I was about to give up, I noticed a small square of paper peeking out from under the drawer liner. It read, Eustis 411 followed by a phone number.

My heart began racing. Eustis was my Daddy's name, and this must be his contact number!

I ran back to my room, and scrawled the number in pen onto the inside waistband of my old jeans that were still sitting in my dresser from the day I arrived, and then started to plan my next move.

The next morning I drove to a pay phone a few towns away, and dialed the exchange. After several rings, he picked up. I finally heard the long lost voice I had been yearning to hear…it was my Daddy!

I nervously hung up the phone though, as my paranoia set in. I could never let Uncle know that I called.

Why had Uncle been keeping us apart all this time, or maybe it was Daddy, maybe he didn't want me in his life anymore.

I was going to play this safe, and in due time, reveal all. I was not going to be defeated, and first on my agenda was to track my Daddy's phone number to an address. I drove home crying tears of happiness from hearing my daddy's voice, but also tears of much disappointment, because I hung up without saying hello.

College

I was accepted to LH University, and decided to live on campus. A great way for me to distance myself from Uncle Daniel. I didn't trust him anymore, and constantly questioned his motive in everything he said or did.

I opened up a private bank account, and every penny I would earn or that Uncle would give me, I would secretly transfer. Going home to Uncle and Aunt Sam's every weekend was difficult though. I did look forward to Church on Sundays, but living on eggshell's, was really taking its toll on me. One day while digging through the old kitchen junk drawer, I came upon a telephone book in which the listings were in the same area code as the first three digits of Daddy's phone number that I had found in Uncle's armoire.

I started with the A's, and patiently followed the numbered listings page by page while I reverently looked for a matching address. Although it was a time consuming task, every spare moment I had, I would process a few more pages.

Several weeks later, my determination would finally pay off, and there in front of me was the match I had been searching for. Daddy was living on a coastal Island that was located two miles offshore from the resort house. With the matching telephone number confirmed, I now knew my Daddy's address and his alias…Mr. Eustis Greene.

 I used to watch over that little Island from the resort house cliffs, and wondered what it was like. So much time had passed, and my Daddy was literally there before me, and even though my outstretched arms could not reach him and my eyes could not see him. He was there! How dare you Uncle Daniel! You have surely met your match this time. I was never able to physically overpower Johnny, but I am powerful in other ways. I will mentally overpower you.

The Wooden Boat

One afternoon, while I was in the den playing with the twins, I overheard a conversation between Uncle Daniel and his local bank. Uncle was trying to salvage the pending sale of the resort house, but the bank confirmed to him there was nothing he could do to save it. The prospective buyer wasn't going to be able to complete the sale due to financing issues.

Uncle needed to start looking for a new buyer. This news actually put a smile on my face, knowing that I could once again freely return to the cliffs, and look over the little Island.

That little Island beyond the cliffs had a completely new meaning to me now. Daddy!

I wasted no time, and soon found myself back at the resort house.

With my binoculars in hand, I watched the yachts disappear in and out of the Island's little harbor that day. I also watched the fishing skiffs as they trolled across the oceans open byway.

While looking beyond the edge of the cliffs one day, I eyed an old wooden boat below, and pondered its origin. It wasn't very big, and it was barely hanging onto the edge of the shore. I became determined to find my way down to the beach below, and diligently cased the property from edge to edge, but could not find a pathway. Not even a remnant of one.

That evening after opening the old trunk from Rose, and studying her many childhood photos for clues, I found what I had been looking for. The vintage sepia photograph that I was staring at, barely showed the narrow path behind her. I put the photo in my purse, and tomorrow I now had a path to find.

I excused myself from the dinner table that Sunday, and told Aunt Sam that I had to get back to the University to study for exams, but soon found myself back at the resort house and with the photo in hand; I started to walk the property's edge again. If I could match the old photo of Rose, to the exact spot where she was standing when it was taken, the path to the shore below would surely be found.

Somewhere behind the old carriage house and at the lowest point of the property, I saw before me a mass of wild beach plums that were tangled within the roots of the unruly yet beautiful wisteria. Carefully parting my way through the snarl of branches, there it was.

It was mostly grown in, but apparent. I cautiously made my way down the clay cliffs, and by the time I reached the bottom, the first thing I noticed was that the little wooden boat that I had been watching earlier, was now gone. It was just off shore.

I grabbed my binoculars, and caught a glimpse of a man rowing steadily away. At first sight, I thought I was only seeing things, but it was my second glance that confirmed it. I recognized him…it was my Daddy.

I watched as he faded into the horizon, and until he became nothing more than a small speck floating on the sea. I then turned my back, and made my way along the beach, and towards the hidden path again; making sure that I stepped in every footprint that my Daddy had left behind in the sand. My memories of Daddy are what always kept me moving forward.

The Fire

It was from the cliffs, when I started to smell the smoke, and by the time I reached the resort house, I could see the flames blazing through the roof. I frantically panicked, and lost my footing, as I tried making my way to get help. My shaking fingers were barely able to dial the Fire Department.

The trucks whizzed by me as I hurriedly made my way back to the burning house.

Uncle Daniel arrived soon after, and hurriedly approached the Fire Chief. He announced to him in his stern voice, that he was the owner of the property. Amid all of the noise, and commotion, I was busy thinking of Rose. If she were not already gone, this certainly would have killed her. I was expecting more emotion from Uncle, but it was as if he were numb to what was unfolding in front of him. Wrapped in a blanket, I again perched myself on top of the cliffs, as I sadly watched her majesty burn to the ground. The painting that I possessed now, was all that was left of the grand resort. I took a moment to bow my head and pray.

I asked myself over and over again that day, why my Daddy might have been on the beach below, and in that little wooden boat.

Perhaps again, my Uncle knew more than he was willing to tell.

Through the smoke, soot, and ashes in the air shone Uncle Daniel, and the Fire Chief walking towards me. I was asked by the Chief, what I was doing on the property, and if I had seen any suspicious activity. I had to think quickly and only answer him with short and direct answers. I made sure not to give him any information about Daddy, and the wooden boat.

I answered innocently as I stared intensely into Uncle Daniel's eyes and said, "I just stopped here on my way back to the University, like I always do". I showed the Chief my binoculars, and told him that I was watching the fishing boats from the cliffs when I smelled smoke in the air. I had not seen or heard anyone.

While having breakfast the next morning, I read the headline of the Daily News. It simply read "Historic Little Harbor Resort Fire, Arson Suspected". I could tell by the way that Uncle was using his fork as a spear that he was agitated, and now I knew exactly what he was hiding.

Daddy

I was barely able to concentrate on my exams the next day, and when all was said and done, I decided not to return to School for the next semester.

 My priority was to get to the little Island, so I could finally talk to my Daddy. Nothing else mattered to me...nothing! Education would have to wait. Aunt Sam and Uncle Daniel were very upset that I would not be returning to the University, and I had to sit through one of their lengthy lectures on the meaning of success, and the importance of further education. I looked at it this way…This young girl from Ukron has come a long way!

The next morning, after Uncle Daniel & Aunt Sam left with the twins, I drove to the pier. My car was quickly ushered onto the waiting ferry. I stood on deck with my eyes closed tightly and prayed as the ocean spray moistened my face.

This was the most important two mile journey of my life.

Once on the quaint little island, I easily found the sea weathered cape house near the shore, but drove by it several times before I had the courage to stop. My hands trembled as I heard his footsteps.

"Shelby"! He yelled from the entryway as I heard him unlocking the door. My Daddy's smile was as big as I remembered it to be, and my heart was so happy that it was ready to burst!

The sight of him was every Christmas and Birthday I had ever had all rolled into one. He picked me up, and swung me around a bit while he lovingly kissed my cheeks. Daddy was thrilled to see me. I was so relieved to feel his comfort and unconditional love again. I never wanted to let go. With a tickle of his mustache, and the smell of tobacco from his shirt pocket, there was no place in this world that I would rather be.

Daddy's smile though, turned quickly to concern and he asked, "Does Daniel know you are here"? With a grimace, I answered no.

I told Daddy how I had located him months earlier, by secretly going through Uncle Daniel's things.

I went on to let Daddy know how I had traced his phone number to his address, and how I had once even seen him rowing away from the shore in that little wooden boat. He smiled at me as he listened, but he had a distinct nervousness about him. We had so much to talk about.

I told him that it had been a very long time since I had been back to Ukron, and how my heart yearned for my Mom, Brad, Flossie, Sarah, and Quinn. Daddy hung his head and told me that Uncle Daniel owed him thousands of dollars, and once he received his money, he would be leaving the Island to head west. He wanted to go back to Ukron too. His heart was also yearning for the same thing as mine.

We immediately found common ground. I made a deal with Daddy that day…If he opened up to me, I would be honest with him in return. It was such a comfort to finally get all of the pain that I had been harboring out into the open with him. To me…Daddy always fixed everything.

I started telling Daddy about Johnny and all of the physical abuse that he inflicted upon me.

I told him about the dead farmer in the Ukron field, and how Johnny had been badly beaten.

Then I talked about Rose, and how her poor little dog Skipper had become very sick and why.

I opened up about the circumstances behind Rose's death, and how I thought Uncle had stolen the resort house from her as motive. Then I told him about the fire. I was very suspicious of Uncle Daniel, and asked Daddy if he were capable of such despicable acts. Daddy paused as he struggled to find the words to answer me. "Shelby, your suspicions could be right".

Daddy confirmed what I thought I already knew, and he went on to tell me that he would never see a penny of the money Daniel owed him unless he did exactly what Daniel said. He assured me that none of his own actions were in vain, and I believed him. But, in fact…it was my Daddy who set the resort house on fire that day. Enough words were spoken…after all Uncle Daniel had been blackmailing him, and was keeping him in hiding. I told Daddy that I had managed to save a substantial amount of money while living at Uncle Daniel's, and that he need not worry.

I promised that I would stay strong, and return to Uncle Daniel and Aunt Sam's house. We also made a pact that I would come back to the Island to visit him once a week. It was difficult to let go of Daddy's hand when it came time for me to go. There was one more promise Daddy asked of me that day. Before we said our goodbyes, he made me promise him that I would go back to the LH University, and finish my degree program.

I arrived home just as Aunt Sam was serving dinner that evening. I was smiling from ear to ear, after having the best father and child reunion ever. At the Dinner table I announced that I was not going to be leaving the University after all. Uncle Daniel showed his approval with his typical pat on the head. I looked up at him, and instead of seeing Uncle Daniel, all I saw was a murderer, arsonist, and blackmailing thief sitting before me. A monster who's approval I would never seek again.

From now on, I would sleep with my back to the wall, and my loving dog Skipper by my side.

Childhood trust starts with a healthy adult/mentor relationship, and ends, not with mistakes, but with poor adult decisions ~

Pain

I awoke early the next morning, and lay in bed while having deep thoughts of my family back in Ukron. My brother Brad was eighteen now. He had always reminded me of my Daddy with his thick dark hair, and lean stature. I could picture him driving through Ukron in my little black sports car with a pretty girl by his side. Flossie was sixteen, and the only redhead in the family. She was usually found wearing her long hair in braids under a big straw hat, while working in the garden. I admire her patience, and her ability to bring life to everything she touches. Sarah fifteen; was a tomboy with spunk. I wondered if she had turned into a swan yet, and my baby sister Quinn, twelve was just that. In my eyes, she would always be the baby and always be protected.

I tried to turn away from my thoughts about Ukron, because every good memory would soon dissipate, and all of the pain that Johnny had inflicted on me over the years would swiftly come flooding back, and take its place.

I had known Johnny since I was twelve years old. He tried to worm his way into my heart when we first met, by trying to win me over with his corny jokes, and his untrusting smile, but as soon as he realized that I could see right through him, everything changed.

My first run in with Johnny came when he asked me to vacuum the parlor rug, but a last minute invitation to join some friends for a walk found me bolting out the front door. Mom gave me her approval to go, and vacuuming for Johnny was the last thing on my mind. I shared a small bedroom with Flossie at the time, and slept on the top of the bunk bed in our room. I was sleeping soundly that night, until his forceful hand abruptly grabbed me by the back of my head. With a quick tug, I was pulled to the floor. I frantically tried to break loose and scramble myself to the bathroom across the hall to lock myself in, but I could not break free from his clutches. I used my hands as a shield to cover my face, while he literally kicked the crap out of me. Flossie alerted everyone in the house as she sharply screamed for help. Johnny repeatedly kicked me in the stomach, his teeth were clenched, and under his breath he chanted, "I hope you will never be able to have children" over, and over again. The entire family was watching now from the hallway. The little ones were all crying, and begging him to please stop. Johnny then dragged me into the parlor by my ankles. I was squirming to get away, but I was no match for him. He directed the family to sit on the couch, and told them to watch as he was going to teach me a lesson. Mom was already sitting in her black rocker, smoking a cigarette. She had the best seat in the house. Johnny yelled, "I told Shelby to vacuum the parlor, and she didn't do it". He was viciously animated with anger. I was being as stubborn as I could by not letting my Mom, or my siblings see me cry. I was kneeling on the rug in front of Johnny's altar, as he forced my head down, and planted my face into the carpet. I never did make it back to bed that night. Johnny had me pick every speck of filthy lint and dirt out of the soiled rug with my teeth. By morning, my eyes were swollen shut, and Mom hid me down in the basement so I did not have to go to school that day. I knew she wasn't protecting me, but protecting Johnny. My Sister Sarah came down to the basement to sit with me after school for a while. As she gently stroked my hair, she and I talked about Daddy, and we both wept.

From that night forward, I couldn't fall into a deep sleep. Not until Johnny's pacing stopped, and I heard his bedroom door shut.

Forgetting to empty the kitchen trash one evening, ended with me waking up to the whole bag of garbage spilled on top of me as I slept in my bed. In his own demented way, he actually thought this was teaching me a lesson. What I did learn was that Johnny was easily provoked.

The Trial

Any thoughts of Ukron and Johnny would leave me now, even if only for a little while. I wiped the tears from my eyes as I hopped out of bed to the aroma of one of Uncle Daniel's home cooked breakfasts, but I was too paranoid to eat it. "What if"? I thought as Skipper sat by my side.

Uncle Daniel had been indicted on arson charges for the fire at the resort house, and I was being called as a key witness. I was sequestered to a small room behind the judge's chamber. I heard the bailiff yell, "All rise", and held my ear to the wooden door so I could hear the defense lawyer speak, and my Uncle's testimony. Uncle Daniel told the court that the resort house had cost him more than it's worth in restoring it, and with the Summer tourist season approaching, he was sure to find another buyer for it. He testified that he was nowhere near the property that day, and that he was home that day while enjoying a family cookout with his loved ones. He asked the court to please note that they could contact and speak to the priest at his parish. He would also attest that he was in church that Sunday morning.

Finally, I was called out of the little room to testify. After placing my hand on the black Bible that was held before me, and promising to tell the truth so help me God, the lies that I spewed that day would have surely put me behind bars, and sent me to hell.

I will repent to my Lord for the rest of my life, and beg for forgiveness.

Uncle Daniel deserved his due, but the love I held for my father outweighed justice, and all rationality that day, and I am still not sure who won…codependency or unconditional love.

I explained to the jury that our family had gone to church that morning, and enjoyed the day together while having a cookout.

I testified that we had been home the entire day.

Yes, I did leave home to head back to the University, and yes, I did stop at the property on the way, but I never went near the resort house that day, and I never once saw or heard anyone as I watched the boats from the cliff above the shore.

Uncle Daniel was acquitted that day, and he knew it was because of my testimony. He hugged me as we left the courthouse. It was over.

A few months later, my Uncle Daniel received a multi-million-dollar settlement from the insurance company that had accused him of arson. A payment for the loss of the resort house.

I visited Daddy the following week, and he told me that Daniel had finally given him his due.

The Long Road Home

I did it! I received a Bachelor of Arts degree
from the University, and stood proudly in my
kelly green robe, with the rest of my LH
classmates. In the audience sat my Aunt Sam,
the twins, and Uncle Daniel. In my mind's eye as
I looked out into the crowd, I also envisioned my
Mom, Brad, Flossie, Sarah, Quinn, and my
Daddy. As despicable as Uncle Daniel
was…none of this would have happened without
him. I was secretly ashamed of myself. How
could I be thanking a narcissistic criminal for
what I had just achieved.

The next day, Daddy and I were busy packing
up our things, and getting ready for our trip back
to Ukron. I had been searching Real Estate
listings. I planned on buying a home when we
arrived. With all of the money I had saved, and
with my new College diploma, a bright future
awaited my family and I back home in Ukron.

Every day was moving so fast. I could tell by the look on Uncle Daniel's face that it was no surprise to him that I was heading back to Ukron. He tried to talk me into staying, and I am sure it was for his own benefit, but he also knew that I had been homesick for too long. I broke the news to him about Daddy too.

I fibbed, and told Uncle that Daddy called the house, and revealed himself because he thought I was Aunt Sam. I confessed that I had been seeing my Daddy on weekends all along, and that indeed he was coming back to Ukron with me. Again, none of this news seemed to come as a surprise to Uncle Daniel. He just listened to me with his head buried into his chest.

The last things I packed were my guitar, my favorite worn out jeans, and my old leather boots. Aunt Sam cried. We couldn't stop hugging each other. Neither one of us wanted to let go. She had become such a dear friend to me, and I promised her that someday I would return, and thanked her.

I had a twin hanging on each one of my legs as I tried making my way to the car. They did not want to let go either. I loved those rambunctious little boys so much! Uncle Daniel smiled, and simply patted me on the head. As he turned to walk away, I saw him wipe a tear from his eye. I looked back at him, and instead of saying goodbye, I whispered to him, "You know who you are". He did not know it yet, but on his dresser, I left him a picture of Rose.

I took my last ferry ride to the Island. Once there, Daddy and I loaded the roof rack of my car with his belongings. In only two days, we would get to see our family once again.

Traveling with Daddy was something I always wanted to do. We drove, and talked, and talked and drove. Much of our conversations were about Brad, Flossie, Sarah, and Quinn. Daddy had not seen or spoken to them in many years, and wondered if they would even remember who he was. I assured daddy that we had always kept his memory alive.

I had not spoken to my Brother and Sisters since I left Ukron years earlier, and although I would call Mom occasionally, I never did stay on the telephone long enough to catch up with my siblings. For all I knew they probably thought that I abandoned them all. Now, I needed to call Mom right away, and let her know that I was on my way. As I thought about her, I wondered if she had changed, or if she would still be sitting in her black rocker. The same way I left her.

We were about 50 miles from Ukron and we pulled into a 24 hour truck stop for breakfast. While sitting at an old red cracked leather booth waiting for our food, I glanced through a free Real Estate sales booklet that someone had left at the table. It was on the last page that I noticed the old white farmhouse. My sprawling twelve room dream home lay on the page in front of me. There was plenty of room for Daddy too, and acres of land for little Skipper to explore. I stepped outside to the pay phone, and called the number on the listing.

The Realtor who answered said that she could meet us at the property in 2 hours time, and gave me the physical address. So we quickly finished our meal, and hit the road again.

As we approached the old farmhouse, it was just as I had pictured. I stood back to study it, and as I took it all in, I pretended that I was Maria Von Trapp and ran my way through the endless field towards the old farmhouse door. The Realtor explained to me that the property had been abandoned, and therefore, we could move right in (even though the Real Estate process was not complete). I signed the papers and wrote a check out for the down payment. Daddy and I spent the rest of the day exploring the house, and unpacking. Skipper was happily romping around in the yard, just as he always did at the resort house. There was so much to do, but things were starting to look up!

I went to bed that evening, but couldn't close my eyes. I was so excited that I would soon be seeing my family the next day, but frightened at the thought of coming face to face with Johnny.

It was rather late when Skipper suddenly started yapping. Someone was knocking at the front door. I ran downstairs, and cautiously peered through the window to see the Ukron Sheriff standing there with his gun drawn. "Shelby Kane"! He exclaimed as he lowered his weapon. "I thought you were a squatter," he said with a chuckle. I smiled, as I extended my hand to him, and invited him in.

We sat at a folding table in the kitchen. I told him that I had just purchased the old house today, and showed him the papers. He said, "Now where does a young girl like you get the money to buy a place like this". I showed him my University diploma, and he was genuinely so happy for me.

I earned the Sheriff's respect that day. He now knew that I was not the "troubled jerk" that Johnny had made me out to be.

I had never engaged in much conversation with the Ukron Sheriff before, but I was sure he was listening to me now. I also knew my Daddy was eavesdropping from upstairs as I was talking to him.

"Sheriff, I am glad you are here" I said to him. I started at the beginning, and told him that in fact it was Johnny who had kicked me down the landing at the town dump. I told him that I left Ukron, because I was a child in fear of Johnny's abusive ways. I told him that Eustis Kane (my Daddy) had never brought harm to anyone, and how Johnny would use his intimidating threats to keep him from us. "Well Sheriff", "I found my Daddy, and he is an honest, decent man…In fact he is here with me right now". "He lives here too," I proudly stated. With that…Daddy came walking down the stairs with his head held high.

The Sheriff stood up, as Daddy approached him to shake his hand. He would not be riding him out of town ever again. Daddy went on to tell the Sheriff more stories of Johnny's abuse.

By the time the Sheriff stood up to leave, he was shaking his head in disbelief, saying that Johnny was now on his watch list. He apologized to me, and told Daddy to enjoy his family. He said that he would never allow Johnny to ever hurt me or any one of us again. He gave me an assuring pat on the back, told me he was happy we were back in Ukron, and let himself out the door. Daddy kissed me on the forehead, and restfully said goodnight.

The Reckoning

The next morning came early. I called mom, and told her that I was on my way. I had Skipper in tow, and off we went. Daddy stayed behind. We thought it best that I let the kids know he was back in Ukron, and then arrange for a visit. I pulled up to the old dusty homestead.

The first thing I noticed was how run down it had become since I had left.

I didn't go straight into the house, but I knocked on the door. It was Quinn, who answered. "Shelby"! She yelled with excitement.

Quinn was at least 4" taller, and she was as skinny as a rail. Her front teeth had come in beautifully, and her dark brown hair was flowing down to her waist. I was then mowed over by Flossie, Brad, and Sarah. We were laying in a giant pig pile rolling around on the ground together, while laughing, crying, and screaming with happiness. I vowed I would never move away from them ever again. Never!

My eyes happened upon the picture window, and yes, there was my Mom watching us through the glass, and she was smiling. This was the first time I had seen her smile since I was a young girl. I jumped up off the grass, and shook the dirt off while rushing into the house to see her.

I didn't hesitate, but I went straight over to Mom, and I hugged her tightly. For the first time ever, she actually hugged me back. I rested my head on her shoulder, and like a baby, I cried.

Every tear that I ever held back came flooding out onto her sleeve that day. Things would be different now I thought. She does love me, and with as much love as she is capable of giving.

I heard Johnny's gruff voice in the distance yell "Shelby"? My stomach started to tremble, and I wanted nothing more than to vomit. I stayed brave though, as I slowly turned around, and there he was. He was seated in his wheelchair, just like an old dog with no teeth, he glared at me. I glared right back at him, and replied in a sarcastic tone "Hello, Johnny"!

I sat on the dingy couch in the parlor, while everyone gathered around me. The kids were asking me questions, and wanted to hear everything that I had to say.

I told them that I had been away at College. "I am educated now," I boasted.

I let them all know that I had just bought the sprawling old farmhouse at the four corners, and I was here to stay. Everyone gasped in awe. I took Mom's hand, looked her in the eyes and said "Mom, I have Daddy with me…he lives with me now".

My siblings started screaming…almost in unison "Can we see him"? "Can we see him"?

I then asked Brad to take the kids outside, so that Mom and I could talk. She sat silently, and the happiness that I had just seen on her face was starting to fade. I thought for a moment, as I was trying to decide what to say to her next. I explained to her…"This isn't about Johnny, Mom", "This is about our family". "Don't you want what is best for Quinn, Flossie, Brad, and Sarah"? "Don't you want them to see Daddy"?

I waited for what seemed like an eternity for her to answer me, and as I watched the tears swell up in her tired black eyes, she quietly answered…"Yes". I reached over and hugged her again.

Glancing outside, I saw Quinn running through the front yard laughing with her baby carriage. She had Skipper dressed up in her baby doll clothes, and was pushing him along, as the two became quick friends.

Brad was calling me to come outside. He was checking out my sports car. I heard him screaming "Oh, Man"! He did have his license and I opened the door, and threw him my keys so he could take a quick spin through the fields that surrounded us. Being home with this dysfunctional family was the best thing that had ever happened to Daddy and I.

I still needed to talk to Johnny. I bravely walked into the kitchen where he was seated in his wheelchair. "Johnny, I am back, and here to stay", I said firmly. "I just bought a farmhouse here in Ukron". "We need to find some sort of common ground if this is ever going to work out".

He was overtaken with anger, and I could tell that he did not like me calling the shots.

I told him that I had already spoken to the Sheriff, and he knew Daddy was with me. Johnny did not speak at first, but stared into the air. To this day, I still cannot figure out exactly what I ever did in my life to spark Johnny's angry tirades.

I walked over to the kitchen sink for a glass of water, and with my back to him, I was stunned to feel the cold steel blade as he poked it against my spine. "You ain't welcome here Shelby Kane," he angrily growled. "You and your Daddy, go back to where you come from"! The blade of the knife pressed deeper as he spoke. I was too frightened to turn around, let alone breathe. I was afraid that if I did, Johnny would surely lunge the sharp blade into me, so I stood as still as possible while he spoke.

Just as I was calculating my next move, I heard a heavy thump, and the sound of the kitchen knife dropping to the floor.

I spun around to see Johnny slumped over in his wheelchair, and my Mom standing over him with a cast iron skillet in her hand. She knocked him out cold. This was the first time that my Mom had ever really defended me. I knew for sure now that Johnny had lost his power. He would never hurt me again, and Mom for the first time in her life had the upper hand.

The Children and I then drove off to visit Daddy. I left Mom sitting in her black rocker. She was still holding the iron skillet in her hand.

We arrived just before sundown, and Daddy, who had been anticipating our arrival, was waiting on the front porch. He could hardly contain himself, as Brad, Flossie, Sarah, and Quinn stepped out of the car one by one. He was overcome with emotion, and while they all huddled around him, we cried.

We had all been waiting for this joyous moment for a very long time. This long awaited reunion was worth everything that we had ever gone through together to get here.

In my young life I had been physically abused, mentally abused, found two dead bodies, and witnessed arson, but now there would be only solace, and kindness allowed in my life. I would also enjoy a new relationship with Mom, and try to put my troubled past behind me. From now on, the future could only hold good things.

I finally felt some freedom! The last thing I did that day was hang Rose's painting of the grand resort house over the fireplace mantle.

Whatever falls on the lives of children leaves an impression ~

The Captain

It was springtime. Daddy was so happy that we were all together again, and had planned this very special weekend knowing that there was going to be an Air show at the Ukron Aviation Field.

It was the day before the Airshow, and we were all outside doing yard work when Daddy first heard the engines. He was a Korean War 1st Marine Vet, and those P-51 Mustangs were singing his hymn. We all hopped into Daddy's new convertible, and within a few minutes we were spectators to what he thought was going to be the prequel to the greatest show on earth.

We enjoyed watching all of the planes arrive while they strategically lined up in the Ukron aviation field that day, and the warplane pilots were especially friendly. One pilot in particular befriended my family, and even invited my little

Sisters to sit with him in the plane's cockpit, while we took pictures.

After Church the next morning, my Daddy circled the Airfield.

He was strategically plotting for the perfect place to park. There were several aviators practicing above us, as the big event was about to take place.

Directly over our heads was a P-51. Suddenly, and without warning, the plane started to descend from above as if it were a propeller seedling from a maple tree.

I thought it was an aerial trick, but my Daddy knew better. He started screaming as if the pilot could hear him..."C'mon Buddy...C'mon Buddy", and then finally rescinded with "He is not going to make it out of this one"! All of this was happening so fast. We watched in terror as the warplane spun out of control. Daddy sped us along the field in his convertible to get out of the plane's fierce descending path, and I remember him hitting his brakes hard as the plane dug itself into the ground. The poor pilot died on impact, and we were all left stunned!

I thanked God that there were no other casualties that day. Over one hundred people had witnessed this tragic event.

Daddy saluted the pilot through the wreckage as we drove by, and to this day...I don't know why I covered my ears, and not my eyes. It was soon learned that the pilot was no other than the friendly pilot who had befriended us the day before. I think of him often. God Bless you Captain.

This was now the third death that I had witnessed, and something that I could not protect my Sisters from as I watched the horror etch itself onto their innocent faces. Now I couldn't even trust myself. If I had not come back to Ukron, I felt that none of this would have happened.

The Breakdown

I wish I could tell you that this was the end of my story, but it was just the beginning. I felt I had risen above a childhood of trauma. I always thought of myself as a survivor, my own personal hero of sorts, after all...I thought I had created a functional life for myself, and defeated all of my abusers, but as time passed on, I felt an overwhelming heaviness inside that I could not shake. There were so many emotions within me, and I could not suppress or control them any longer.

All of those years of remaining strong and resilient did not follow me into adulthood like I thought it would. This time I was trapped, as if I was truly losing control of myself.

I became very withdrawn, and started living within my head. I was being haunted by flashbacks from my past, and still at night I would see the face of that dead farmer in the field, Rose, and now the Captain and his Plane. It was relentless! I would still see the flames from the old resort house, and sometimes I would even pick at my arms as if I were picking out shards of glass as a result of one of Johnny's narcissistic outbursts at the Ukron town landfill. I would tell myself that I was safe, but it only made my thoughts become more profound, and ruminating. It took no time at all for the physical symptoms, and sensations to take center stage in my life, emotionally and physically this all became too much for me to handle. I was exhausted.

I decided to see a CBT Therapist to get some much needed therapy, and after many sessions discussing my childhood trauma, I underwent hypnosis to help pinpoint the original root causes of my newly diagnosed PTSD, Generalized Anxiety Disorder, and Health Anxiety. Initially, I couldn't help but reject the thought that connecting with my "inner child" would help me to heal. I actually thought it was all a bit hokey at first, but eventually I started to embrace, and connect with little me through my subconscious mind. I needed to reconnect, and reframe my past in order to heal. Reprogramming how my subconscious responds, and learning to accept and trust was key!

I had kept, and held on to so many childhood secrets, and so much pain over the years, I couldn't deny that this was a catalyst that led me on the path to where I was today.

The body and mind are connected. When our limbic system overloads, it expresses itself with its need to get our full attention. It will outweigh all logic to boldly protect you, not only emotionally, but also physically. No matter how uncomfortable, these persistent alerts are meant to keep us safe, and keep our sole attention to avert any perceived danger.

"Anything the mind can cause, the mind can heal" ~ Dennis Simsek

The Stay

I was absorbing all that I was learning about myself, and spending each day trying to accept, and trust my diagnosis. I in fact had an anxiety/health anxiety disorder with PTSD leading the way. I was starting to find myself in my bed most of the time, and I was still retreating from all daily interactions as a result of how I was feeling. One morning I awoke, and while trying to stand I fell to the floor, and had to crawl to the bathroom. I was so dizzy that I was unable to walk. This is what finally put me over the edge.

I shopped several doctors, and hospitals looking for a different diagnosis, but I was always sent away while being assured that it was indeed anxiety. I never did find the reassurance I was looking for, and it dug me in deeper, which kept me in survival mode.

My family who I loved so dearly, and who I had always lovingly nurtured, were now nurturing me…all but my Mom.

That was when the epiphany happened, and it all clicked. I was never nurtured as a child by my own mother, and because of this, the help from a loved one now, was very difficult for me to accept. I craved for once in my life…"to be loved without a motive".

All of this had been caused by a childhood full of trauma, neglect, and the lack of being parented. It was very overwhelming, and confusing, and hearing this did not take away what ailed me.

I thought I had put all my trauma behind me when I came back to Ukron, but realized that you can't quickly put behind you what has been buried so deeply in your subconscious mind for your entire life, and especially when it is hiding. Patience, acceptance, and staying mindful would get me there, but in the meantime…anxiety persisted to call me.

The trauma that I held was barely floating to the surface. Healing is very painful!

24/7 daily, and chronically. I felt no better. I in fact felt it was worsening, and I became steadily more secluded and symptomatic.

My Psychotherapist suggested that perhaps I should will myself into an inpatient psychiatric facility for respite. I was so desperate for relief from my broken down self that I agreed, and signed the papers that would subject me to what I thought would be three days of evaluation, and mental health support.

When the facility door opened the odor was the first thing that sensitized me. A combination of human urine, feces, and old food trays whiffed through the hallway. I closed my eyes as I hesitantly stepped over the threshold. I was met by a medical doctor, and a nurse who frisked me and took all of my personal belongings away.

My wrist was wrapped with a paper ID bracelet, and then they even took the shoelaces out of my shoes.

I thought that I had done nothing wrong, and how dare they treat me in such a callus, and uncaring way. I was just there to get help…"What were they seeing in me that I could not see in myself"? I was devastated!

As I was being led past a sitting area, all of the other patients were intently watching my arrival as I walked towards the room that I would be occupying. I spoke only when spoken to. I needed to get through the humiliation of this insidious experience.

Patients were allowed outdoors for 15 minutes three times a day after our cafeteria meals, and other than that there was nothing to do but pace the floors, and like a tiger in a cage, I did just that! This led to my hyperstimulation, and psychomotor agitation.

I paced back and forth as I watched adults splatting wet diapers on the floor, while some others stood in the hallways screaming. Many were so far off in space that they didn't even know where they were due to their high doses of psychiatric medication.

I hid as many tears as I could so that I was not approached to swallow a pill from a little white dixie cup. There was no counseling, and no support at all, and I felt as if I had been duped.

There was one nurse there who read my fear, as I also read the kindness on her face. She invited me to sit with her during lunch break so we could talk.

The remainder of my time was spent self guarding myself from the other patients, and that nurse? She insisted that I share my cafeteria and outdoor time with her, and the staff. By the time I left that facility, I was no better at all. It was just another traumatic experience, and when I was finally released and getting ready to walk out the door with my shoelaces in my hand,

I was handed a big bottle of pills, and sent home with the same diagnosis I had heard before. PTSD, Generalized Anxiety Disorder, and Health Anxiety.

I was now officially certified, and felt that I was leaving with a diploma of sorts, and one that could not be celebrated. One that labeled me as an official mental health patient forever.

My head hung towards the pavement as I walked to the car. That facility had torn me down...not only by what I witnessed while I was within its walls, but also from the faces of the many patients that knew no different. When I arrived home again, I felt I had earned my freedom, and I was happy and relieved to see my family, but I could not stop wondering if the people around me could see my new indelible mental health reminder. The one that I thought I would never be able to wash away.

No More Secrets

During my toughest days I was very bitter inside, and I would tell myself continually that I was just a jerk, a liar, and not worth the air that I breathed.

I couldn't control my compulsiveness, while ruminating my every thought, from the moment I awoke each morning, and anxiously awaited the evening so I could finally close my eyes again and forget it all.

I Never gazed into a mirror without seeing an ugly, and angry little girl before me who just wanted to be loved, but had not yet learned how to love herself. A very distorted outlook, and I know now, even though I didn't recognize it then, that I could not hide from myself anymore. No more secrets. Being a spiritual person I prayed, and in a pious way, I prayed like I never had before. Dear Lord, don't let me lose control of myself or reality...ever, Amen.

I did some reading about Generational Trauma, and due to the lack of my own parental nurturing, realized that I had a secondary gain to my health anxiety. One that unconsciously had me living my life with a victim mentality.

I was also schooled by my CBT Therapist that my physical symptoms, and health anxiety were a result of this. A personal shield to protect myself from all future harm. A form of malingering that kept me in a frozen state, and full of excuses that kept me from moving forward.

I dug even deeper as I read every book I could find on the subject of anxiety and psychological healing. I became very frustrated with it all, because although I was learning so much, I still wasn't feeling any physical or mental changes. I had no positivity at all.

I continued staying within the comfort of my home like a prisoner, and watched my little sports car sit in the yard from afar, just wishing I had the courage to drive it again. "Only if I were not dizzy"! There was always something or someone to blame for my failure to take that first real step. I was subconsciously sabotaging my own efforts, and for every positive thought, a dozen negative thoughts would take its place. Climbing out of this hell hole without a ladder would be the hardest thing I had ever done.

Anxiety makes you feel like you are dying every moment of every day, and it continues to rotate, like a carousel that plays the same music, and never slows down enough to give you the opportunity to jump off. Not even in your dreams.

Anxiety manipulates your every thought, and holds you in the grips of hell. It also grasps at you even harder, the more you beg for mercy.

I Matter

One morning I awoke, and it wasn't the clouds that I saw when I opened my eyes, but the sun peeking through my drawn curtains. A bright ray of light, and I took it as a sign. I stepped outside with my headphones on, and a cup of coffee in my hand. I took in the soft breeze as I sat on my porch swing and shut my eyes.

I started listening to the pioneers of psychology, and their healing methods, through the audio books of Claire Weekes, Erich Fromm, Dennis Simsek, and Bessel Van Der Kolk.

My baby sister Quinn soon joined me, and I was about to be taught one of the greatest life lessons yet. This curious wide eyed little girl opened up to me and asked me "What do you do when you love someone, and no matter what you do…they don't love you back"?

Several of my life experiences started rushing through my brain, but my response to her was simple. I said "Accept it". It is our own lives that matter. Never judge your wins or failures on the merits or opinions of others, but take responsibility for yourself. Wake up everyday with a sense of self love, self worth, and never set your standards so low that anyone makes you feel that you are worthless or unloved. The truth is that they don't deserve your love. Be true to you, and know that everything you are to yourself will also reflect in every aspect of your life. So always love who you are. Trust in your own judgment, and especially on your instincts.

I then embraced Quinn in such a loving way, and it was as if I were also embracing my own inner child. Truly trusting and accepting myself was exactly what I was missing in order for me to heal. Putting myself first without the reliance of someone else's love or approval. A true unconditional love for me!

That day Quinn brought a smile to my face. We sang a few Church hymns together as we drifted back and forth on the porch swing.

This led me to another revelation. I needed to talk to my Mom. I needed to find out what her childhood was like, and connect the dots from her past to mine. What type of Generational Trauma has she harbored all of these years?

You are never too old to talk to your past ~

The Revelation

The next morning after a cold shower, I wandered over to my sports car, hopped in and turned the key. I called this a big win because I did this freely, and without a thought. As I ventured down the old gravel road toward Mom's house I kept repeating the words of Thich Nhat Hanh…"*With every step, I arrive at my destination*".

Mom seemed happy to see me, and as we sat across from each other and smiled, I had a sense that I had caught her in a mood that would enable me to delve deep into her past. What I didn't expect was Mom's eagerness to open up to me, and spill it all!

Mom was the only daughter of six children. Imagine having five brothers! Her mom, (My Nana) and her dad (My Papa) were both hard working, and would rely solely on my Mom to take care of her siblings on a daily basis.

This not only involved caring for, but also daily household chores, and cooking. Living in a small mill workers home was not easy for my Mom growing up, and being tied down as a small child to a house full of boys was near impossible, is how she explained it.

I listened intently as she spoke, and her own traumas started stacking up in my head as if they were my own. One that took me back was when she spoke of how she had to share a room with her brothers, and how they would sneak over to her bed during the night and molest her. It was then that I let her know that I had also been molested by one of her brothers when I was nine years old. I never said a word about it before, because I was so afraid that my Daddy would have found out. It surely would have made the outcome a lot worse.

Why would she leave me as a child with her predators if she knew what they were capable of? "Trying to heal the "Mother Wound" is hard work" I thought deeply, as I held my composure, and cried to myself. None of this was my fault!

A Child should never blame themselves for the actions of their elders ~

Mom also spoke of my Nana and Papa, and how they would make her stand while barefoot with her little toes positioned under the rocking chair rungs. They would then rock over her toes if she misbehaved or did not finish her chores. My Nana would also hit my Mom over the head with an old cast iron pan too. Now I know why Mom chose that as her weapon of choice the day she challenged Johnny in the kitchen.

My Mom had spent her entire life as a codependent and normalized it. She knew no different! Mom then generationally passed this down into the lives of her own children.

She never knew how to love, because she was never nurtured or shown love herself.

Our visits became more frequent, and each time we spoke, Mom would open up more of her past to me.

I can remember sitting across from her one day, and wondering how she survived it all, and realized that her whole life was spent in survival mode too. I connected, and confirmed to myself at that moment that I in fact, was just like my Mother.

So this is how Generational Trauma continues from one generation to the next. At that point, I knew that when I eventually married and had children, that my children would be nurtured, loved, and that I would do my best to end, and leave Generational Trauma behind for good.

I never let up on my healing journey, and continued to attend CBT Therapy, and Wellness Classes daily. I also furthered my education in Psychology.

Healing doesn't happen overnight. Healing hurts…It takes a lot of very hard work and dedication to recondition the neuroplastic brain.

By acknowledging and befriending my trauma, it made me brave enough to finally trust…to allow myself to feel while discovering what was below the surface of my past, and also my ancestral past. There are so many healing lessons to learn while letting it go. Connecting with my inner child, also allowed me to break through, and truly love myself again… unconditionally!

Trying to heal while going through the motions, and without real intention is like trying to row a boat without a paddle.

With Childhood abuse and trauma, there is no age of reason. It is only when the adult child realizes that they are the only ones who can rescue themselves, do they then start to heal ~

Update

It has been just over 20 years since I moved back to Ukron with my Daddy. My days here have been the happiest days of my life.

I became a local Writer, a Christian CBT Life Coach, and NLP Practitioner.

I met my husband Jake, and we married after a whirlwind romance, and have two children, David, and Aine.

My Daddy sadly passed away of pancreatic cancer at the age of 67. I am so happy that his days in Ukron were the best days of his life too. We were all by Daddy's bedside when he took his final breath.

Brad, Sarah, Quinn, and Flossie still live in Ukron, and are all fully College educated too.

Mom still lives in the old farmhouse with Johnny. Her independence has bloomed, and she even drives over to visit me now and then. Mom no longer spends her days in that black rocker.

My husband Jake and I went back to the East Coast for our anniversary last year, and we took a ride to the cliffs where the old resort house once stood, and I broke down. I told Jake the story of Uncle Daniel, and about what happened to poor Rose. I had never talked to anyone about this before except for Daddy. No one ever!

I made one last stop that day. I went to see my Uncle Daniel, and Aunt Sam. I knocked on their door, and it was Aunt Sam who answered. She double-took when she saw me, and yelled for Uncle Daniel. They were both quite aged now, and the house run down.

We talked about Daddy, and the twins. Uncle never did come to Ukron to pay his respects when Daddy died.

When Jake and I were leaving, Uncle patted me on my head just as he always did, and Aunt Sam hugged me tight. I knew I would never see them again as I walked away, and never looked back.

To this day when I think about Uncle Daniel, I also think of Rose, and how he got away with it.

Today I look back upon my journey of self discovery, and healing…A journey that is mostly behind me now, and a journey that saved me. I will never stop growing, learning, and will always live my life with a new type of strength. Not one of resilience, but one made of acceptance, self love, forgiveness, and trust. I have finally learned to live in the moment

Writing this has revealed to me just how far I have come.

~Shelby Kane~

NOTES